Dear Tracy

thanks for

keeping me

Safe

Love from

Sarah

The moral right of the authors has been asserted. A catalogue record of this publication is available from the British Library.

First published in Great Britain in 2021

ISBN 978-1-8380546-4-9
A Motiv8.me publication

Motiv8.me Press
Wrexham Enterprise Hub
11-13 Rhosddu Road
Wrexham
LL11 1AT

www.motiv8.me

MOTIV8.me

The Family
An Anthology of Psychosis

Dr Sarah Mackay PhD

"You are here to enable the divine purpose of the universe to unfold. That is how important you are!"

-Eckhart Tolle

Contents

Acknowledgements

This anthology is dedicated to my two favourite people who have been with me throughout my journey. Tom and Naomi. Thank you for being here with me. I love you so much. I also write in the memory of my late professor, Alex Carson, who had every faith in me.

I want to thank Allan, my editor, for recognising and seeing the potential in my manuscript. I also want to thank Mary Mangus, Emma Wrigley, and Melissa Dohnal who read through the early drafts and cheered me on from the sidelines.

Foreword

The therapeutic outlet of poetry and art is poignantly depicted in Dr. Sarah Mackay's courageous journey with psychosis. Sarah's anthology touches me as a book that will strike a chord and reach out to those who have experienced that deep, intense struggle with mental ill health and darkness, as well as light.

The illustrations speak for themselves as both an emotive and spirited accompaniment to her words.

Beginning with the delightful heartfelt poem 'Honey' which introduces us to Sarah's world, the reader finds themselves by her side in the darkness of 'The Family', 'Triggered', 'Fetid' and 'Fake' with more poems leading us through to the warming conclusion and solace of 'The Prayer'. Also, for therapists and those interested in art and poetry as therapy, this beautiful gift of sharing from Sarah can't fail to open hearts and minds and bridge the gap for those who have felt isolated in their distress.

Emma Sims
Author, 'Self-Care for Givers and the Helping Professions'

Foreword

Voice hearing is a common human experience. Many people hear voices. It is a real experience. There may be many different unique experiences that people have of voice hearing. Studies have found that between 4 and 10% of people across the world hear voices. Simply put, hearing something that others around aren't. Voices can be encouraging and helpful or may be frightening, critical, threatening or commanding.

We both work as Mental Health Nurses/PSI Specialists (psychosocial intervention) for the NHS and have a passion for working alongside people who are struggling with voice hearing experiences, or other unusual experiences. We facilitate a Hearing Voices Group in Wrexham, North Wales and this is where we met Sarah, author of this book.

The first UK Hearing Voices Network (HVN) was founded in Manchester in 1988, following on from the original HVN founded in the Netherlands in 1987 by Dutch Psychiatrist Marius Romme, the science journalist Sandra Escher and voice hearer Patsy Hage. One of the roles of the HVN is to offer support to and help develop local Hearing Voices Groups (HVG). Our Wrexham group is affiliated to HVN Cymru.

The ethos of the group is of self help, mutual respect and empathy. As with other HVGs, it is a self help/support group, not a therapy or treatment group. We believe that learning to live with voices successfully is an achievable outcome and may be more realistic for some people than getting rid of voices. We do not regard voices as a meaningless experience so that the only beneficial outcome would be to stop them completely. Group members have a space and the opportunity to talk openly about the voices, visions or other unusual experiences with the aim of helping each person understand what is happening in the context of their own life experiences, which can, as a consequence, reduce some of the fear and anxiety that might be felt.

A theme of the group is of compassion. Compassion for self, others and for the voices. We employ principles of Compassion Focussed Therapy (CFT, Paul Gilbert) and CFT for Psychosis (Charles Heriot Maitland) of which there is plenty of literature to be read, but basically the main drive of CFT is to develop the capacity for self-compassion and self-kindness, which can then stimulate our evolved affect and relationship system, reducing our 'threat' system and increasing our self sooth and drive systems. An aim of the group is to help people develop a different power relationship with their voices. As Sarah describes in this book, the window for her changing the relationship with her voices was found in the Arts. She started to paint her voices, who she knows as The Family. This along with poetry helped her to shift some of the fear and feeling of being controlled, to acceptance and feeling of being more in control. The images and words in her book do not hold back on the pain and fear she has felt, but also hold her hand along her way to her brighter future, living alongside The Family, bringing in colour and hope for a more harmonious life together.

We hope this book will help others who might be struggling with voices, visions or other unusual experiences, find reassurance and hope and find their own window in which to explore their experiences, find some of the meaning linked to those experiences and discover new ways to accept and live with their own equivalent to The Family.

Caroline David and Tony Scannell
- PSI Nurse Specialists, NHS Trust Community Mental Health Team and Facilitators, Wrexham Hearing Voices Group.

Preface

Once I was a wolf. I couldn't communicate normally as I was locked in another realm. I was in a hospital. I met another wolf. And we sat on the floor and talked in wolf language. He was sad because he had lost his brother. The staff could not communicate with him. He only talked in wolf.

I've been in and out of hospital my whole adult life, plagued by The Family. The Family is a group of people that live in an alternate universe. In a place full of demons. I hear them talking to me and talking between themselves. This anthology is our story.

My name is Sarah and I have bipolar with psychosis. Once upon a time I was a nurse, after earning a first-class nursing degree and graduating top of my class. I went on to receive a scholarship to study autism at doctoral level. My work was on the social reproduction of autism. I gave a group of young people video cameras to tell me their stories using a number of prompts. Then I transcribed the videos and analysed the data to create a new story about how autism becomes a social construction. Children are taught how to be autistic. Then the method of treatment, instead of looking at the individual's narrative, is to teach them how to be normal.

My psychiatric journey began as a teenager. I would wake at five in the morning and race up and down the towpath bursting with energy. And then other times, depressed, I would fall asleep in class, on the bus, in the hay barn. I was obsessed with my pony. I loved her so

15

much. She was my solace from the harsh world. My best friend and my confidante.

I started having psychotic episodes during my early twenties. I started hearing voices. Judith, the bossy one, a teenage sulky boy and a baby girl who would cry a lot and seemed really angry. During psychosis you become part of the universe, and the energy flows and you find yourself on a pathway. The voices were on a mission. They wanted me to take them to a safe place. I watched Horton Hears a Who on repeat and it gave me constant messages about my mission. I received messages on sweet wrappers, tv, radio, the bible. I had to save The Family. But I did not know how. So I started painting them. And painting them slowly gave shape to the characters. Judith, the boy, and the baby. The rest were demons that laughed in running water and sometimes were in my body. Sometimes I have a demon in my arm or my stomach. I couldn't quite see The Family at first so painted muffled shapes. I went to visit a friend in Edinburgh

and we went to the Museum of Childhood where I promptly had a panic attack. But I found Snufkin and little My from the Moomins by Tove Jansson, and from then on I used these characters to give shape and structure to my paintings. The clearer the paintings, the easier it was to deal with the voices that were constantly telling me I had to drink bleach to kill the demon in my stomach. For a while I did believe I had a demon in my stomach. So I started playing around with context.

The Family, as they were now known, were taking shape. I painted their miserable faces but I always painted a sunshine or a rainbow as a symbol of the safe place we were heading for. I painted them amongst the flowers and beneath huge rainbows.

Nothing would change their grumpy mood though the baby cried less. They still tell me to do things. Currently they are stuck on wanting me to jump from a road-bridge, which I've absolutely no intention to do. They just put the idea in my head and push and push it. They told me they had killed a lady and her baby. Walked off a cliff top. I saw it on the news and The Family said they did it. I was very scared of them at first but I got used to them. I started painting my real family into the pictures. For example, on the title page my real family are represented by the fish in the water. I also draw a lot of trees because of a preoccupation with seeking shelter.

I am an ordinary person. I have two grown up children and two dogs. I hope you find this narrative to be inspirational. Everything passes. And the universe or God or whoever is always waiting to help you out.

The Family
An Anthology of Psychosis

Dr Sarah Mackay PhD

Honey (aged 12)

I love my little pony
Her name is Honey Bunch
I like to take her for a walk
'cause I love her so much
When I try to catch her
She's three feet deep in mud
If there's a chance to nip me
I'm telling you she would
But even if she's kicking
Or biting at my bum
I love my little pony
And she is my best chum

Despair

What do you see kid, in the valley of despair?
I know you are hurting, believe me, I care
I let you down and for that I am sad
I made you feel dirty and shameful and bad
I don't have the answers, I don't have a plan
I can't promise much but there's someone who can
So take my hand and we'll go there together
Where safe hands will protect us for now and forever

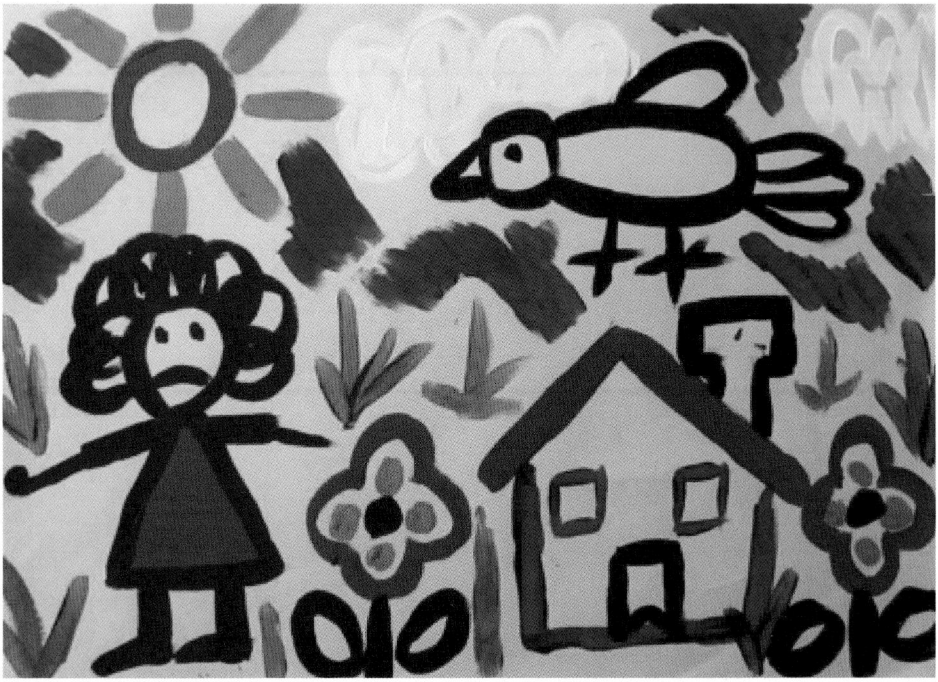

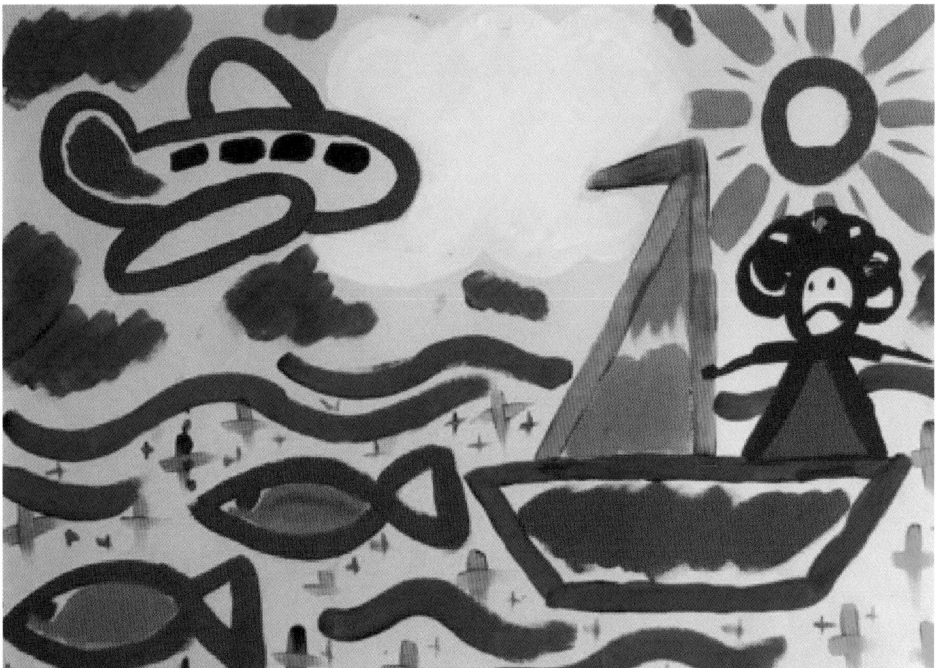

Friends

The world was dark
With murky clouds
While honesty slept above
The truth will out
But will it come
When I have had enough
With ears stopped up
And eyes tight shut
My foggy brain on hold
The world seems bleak
Don't understand
Exactly what I'm told
But with my friends I'll get along
And prove I am not mad
I'm glad they're here to light the way
Without them I'd be sad

The Family

What must it be like
To own your own mind
To not have the voices
That are sometimes unkind
I'm never alone
'though often they're bad
Judith is bossy
The baby is sad
Jump off a road bridge
Often I hear
They push the idea
Increasing my fear
There's a demon in my stomach
Drink bleach they say
Do what it takes
To make it go away
I give in to the meds
To quiet the family
Have my head to my self
Send the demons away

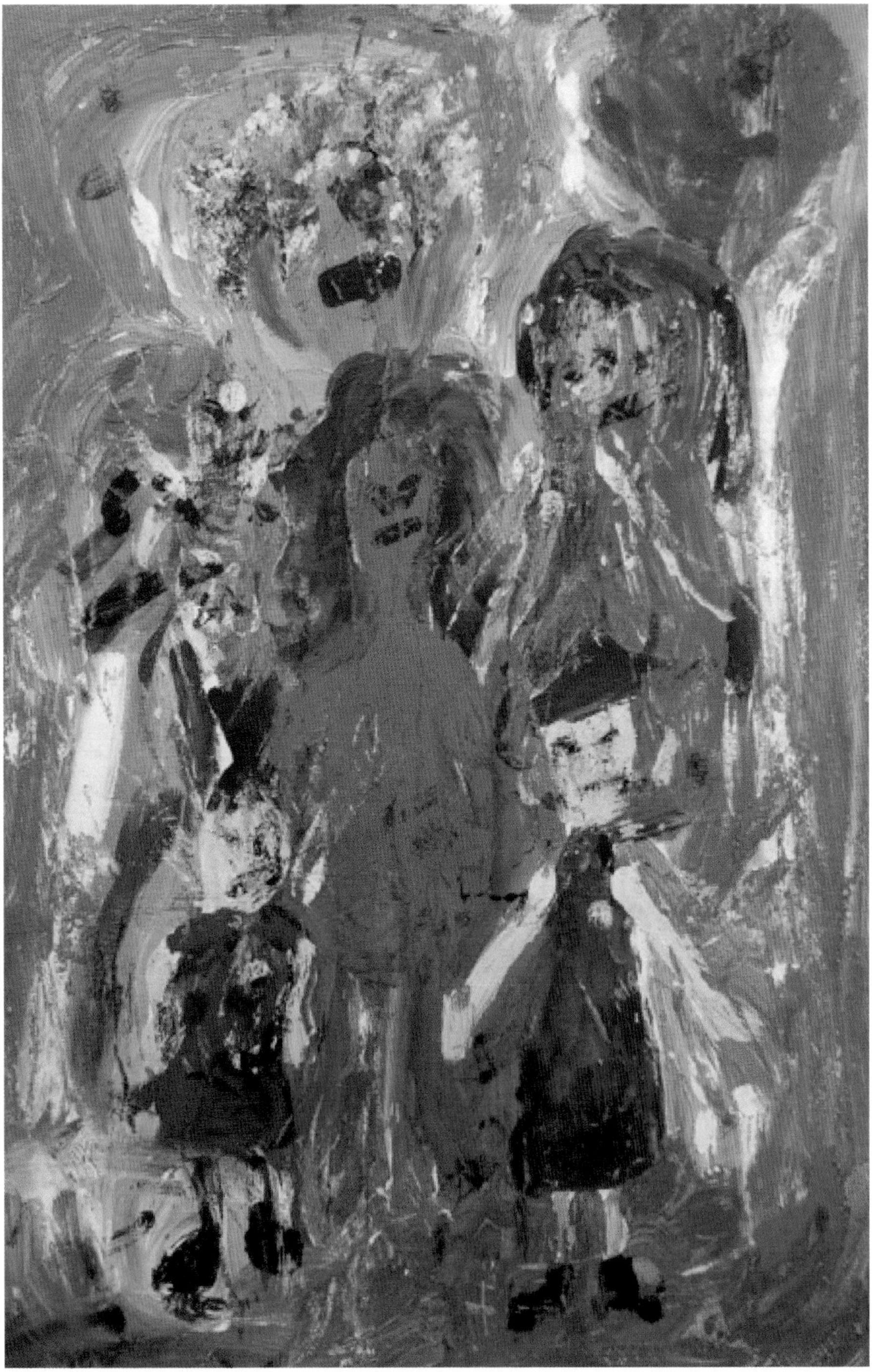

Demon Strike

White hot
Demon strike
Lie awake
Quick like
Take offence
Feel pain
Ever ready
Searing gain
Time's occurring
Moving clearly
Taken lightly
Loved dearly
Bones aching
Time will tell
Buried deeper
Ring the bell
Feel the fear
Instant pride
Taking over
Blue inside

Triggered

Happenings. It leaks through the coating I paint
Chips
Cracks
I wait. Sit and wait. Plot my escape
And become ever more entangled in this life I don't belong to
It's not mine. It's not mine. I didn't ask for it. I don't want it.
It doesn't fit me
I am growing
Shedding the evil robes. They pull and scratch and claw
Threaten to throttle.
Weak I am. And bad. And should be left to die.
Chew off my leg I won't
Gnaw my way to freedom. For what?
Freedom to grow slick black oil of badness once more?
Burn it all away. Red robes. Flame. Blood robes
Your tears won't douse these flames
Weak. Keep your sadness
Keep your madness
Sit and plot
No escape

The Family

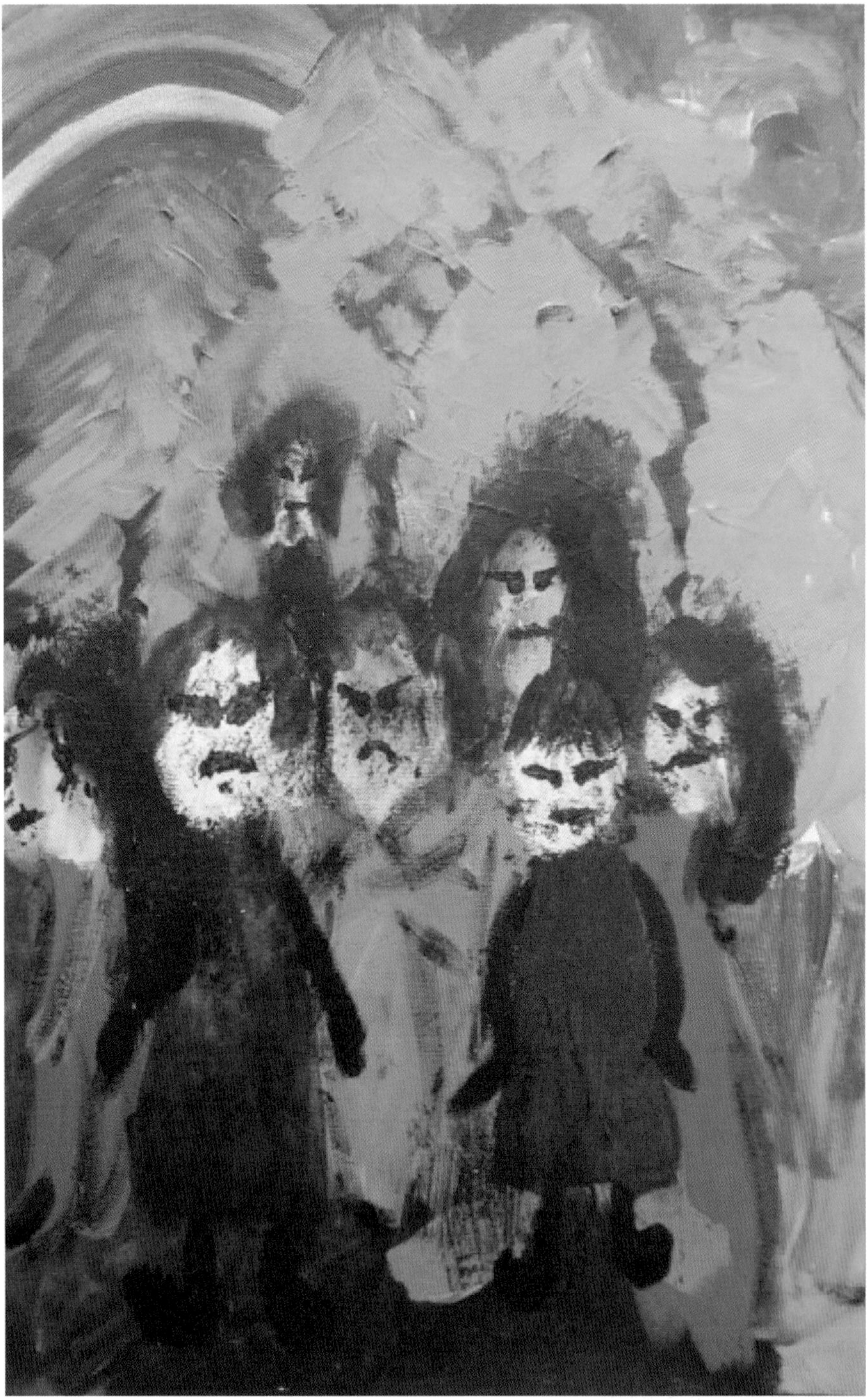

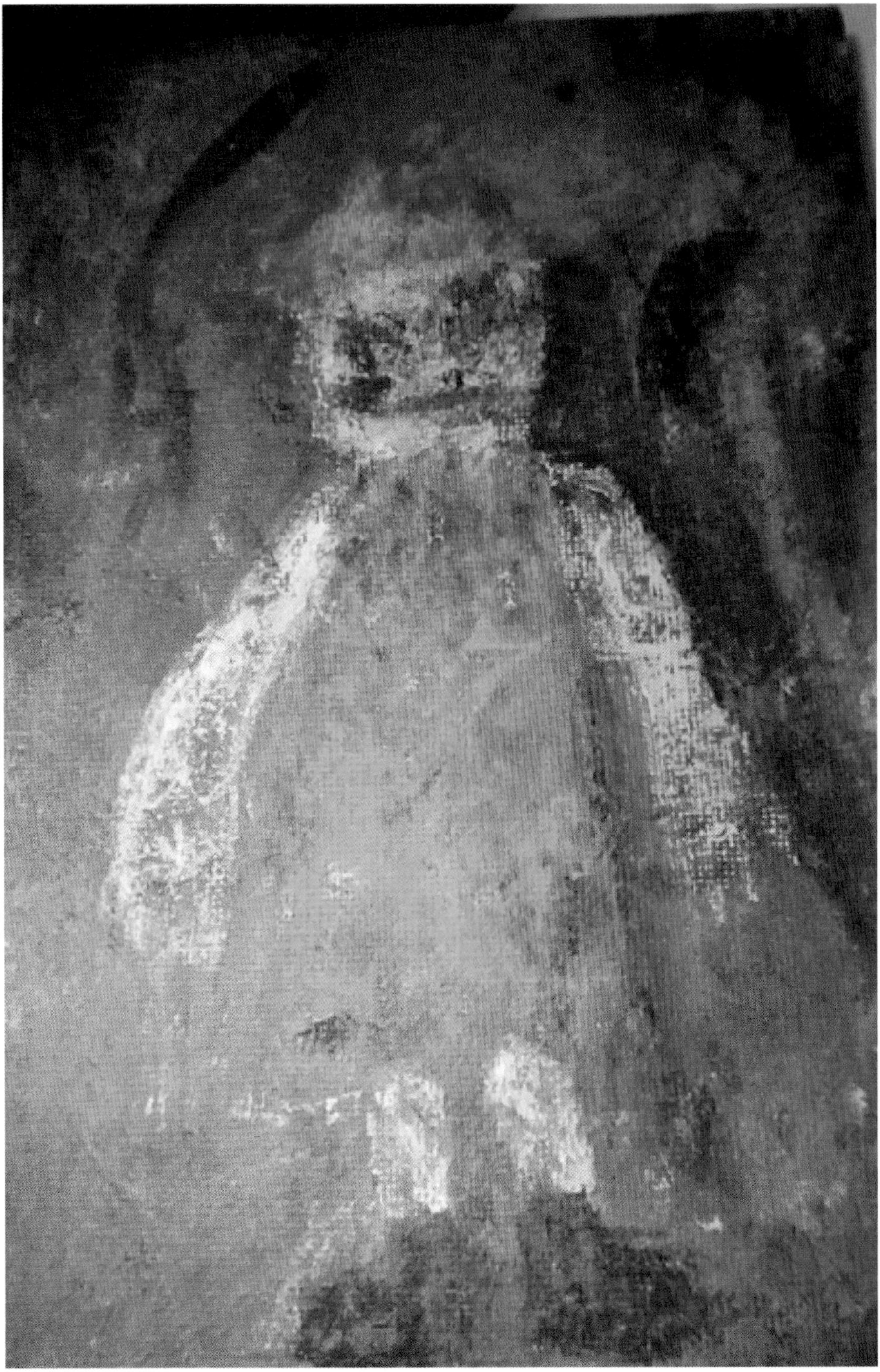

Trapped in Love

You poke me and you prod me
Then you steal away my eyes
You cut me and you burn me
And only ever tell me lies
You bleed away my soul
And you drain away my pride
You leave me feeling helpless
And tell me there's no place to hide
You look at me with anger
All your features burn with rage
You use your strength and power
To keep me trapped inside this cage
You deal out pain and punishment
But say your love is strong
Your fury leaves you saddened
Because you know that it is wrong
At times you are a loving friend
In whom I can confide
But still I wish to be free of
The violence which I bide

Fetid

Heavy
It stirs. Gasping air writhing free
Tendrils torn entails born
From death. From birth. That place so wrong so torn so
Blank
Sewn. Hole. Whole. So

Fetid

It grieves for lust and lusts for breath
Beginning wrong. Bad song. Earth cries and covers her eyes
The shame
Marked

Scream. Stirs. Ground zero. Returns.
Flame-proof fire-proof scorched and black
No exit so shallow. Bed made

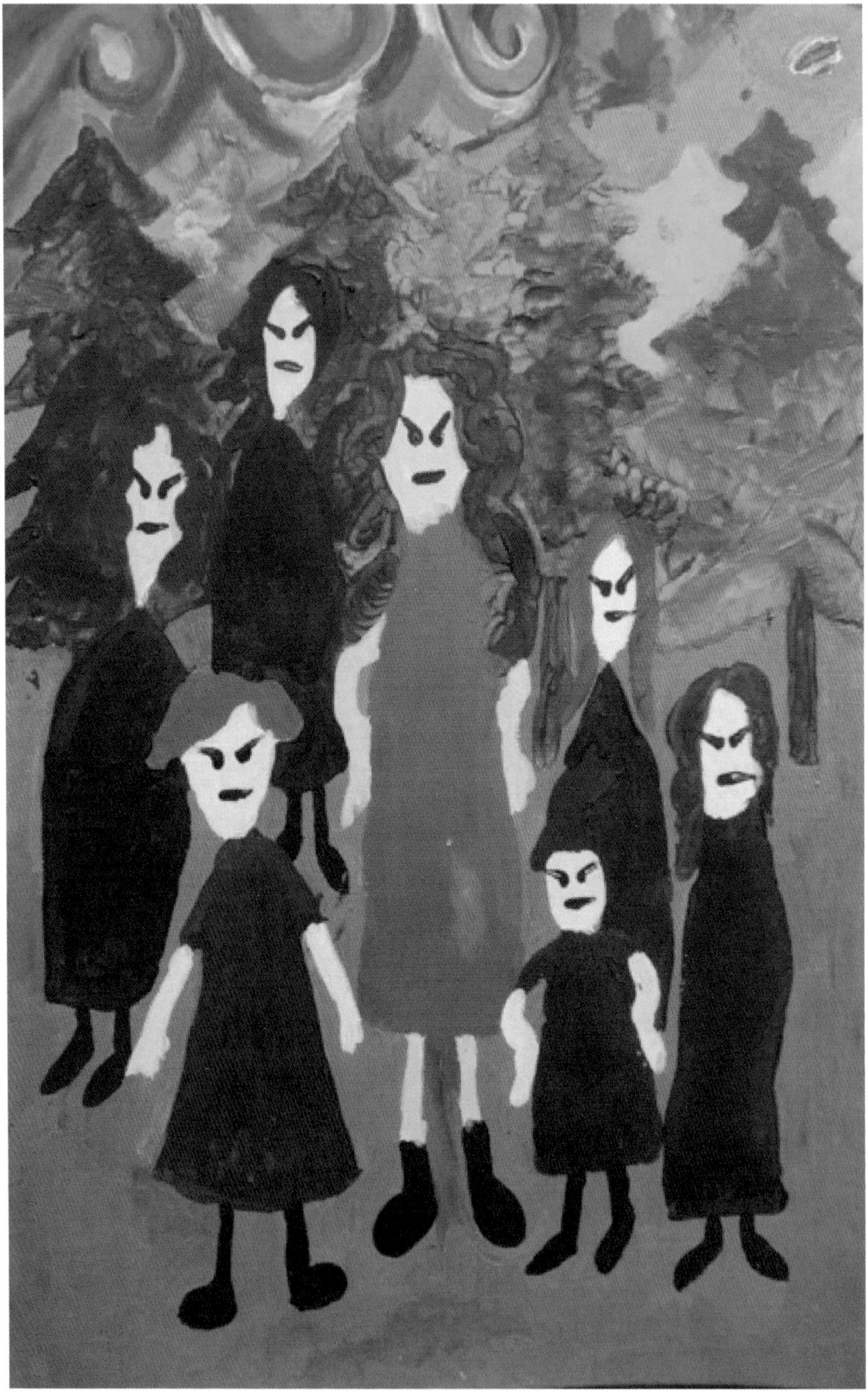

Chatter

They don't care
Won't care. Can't

No escape. I can't die
I see it all
They pretend. And I see through their pretence
Pretention. Pre-tension. Protection
I see through them
I see their lies and torrents of torment
Keep it safe

I WON'T. I can't
I care

It won't let go
I wish I was dead
I wish it was dead. I wish it into the pigs. Demon thing

They are mine and I am its
And I am more fit for swine in this world

We will fight this out. Me and it. And they will rattle no more chatter
RATTLE NO MORE FUCKING CHATTER

Breathe

Trapped she saw
She'd been before
A cage of her own making

Big breath in
The perfect din
Can stop a heart from breaking

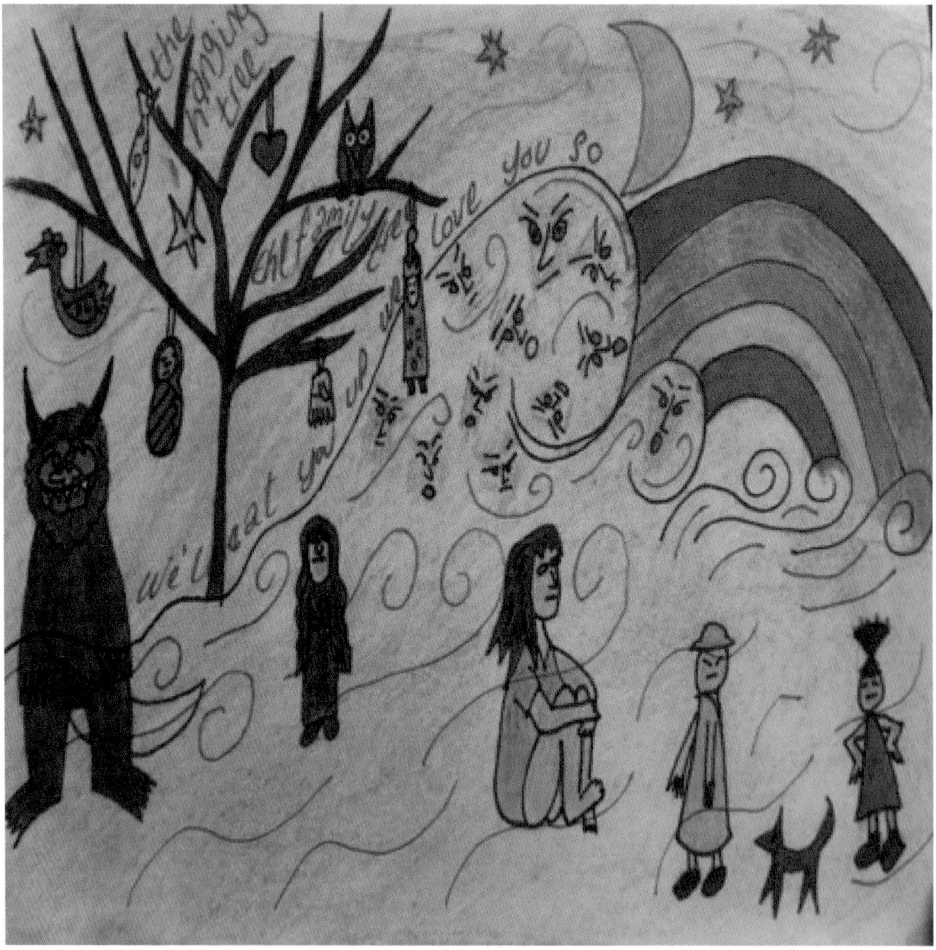
the hanging tree
love you so

Chatter

In the shower
In the rain
Voices chatter
Scream in pain

Laugh in bubbles
Dance with glee
All the time
They pester me

Fear is rising
No way out
Sing in water
Yell and shout

Turn away
Stay awake
Voices chatter
Jump and shake

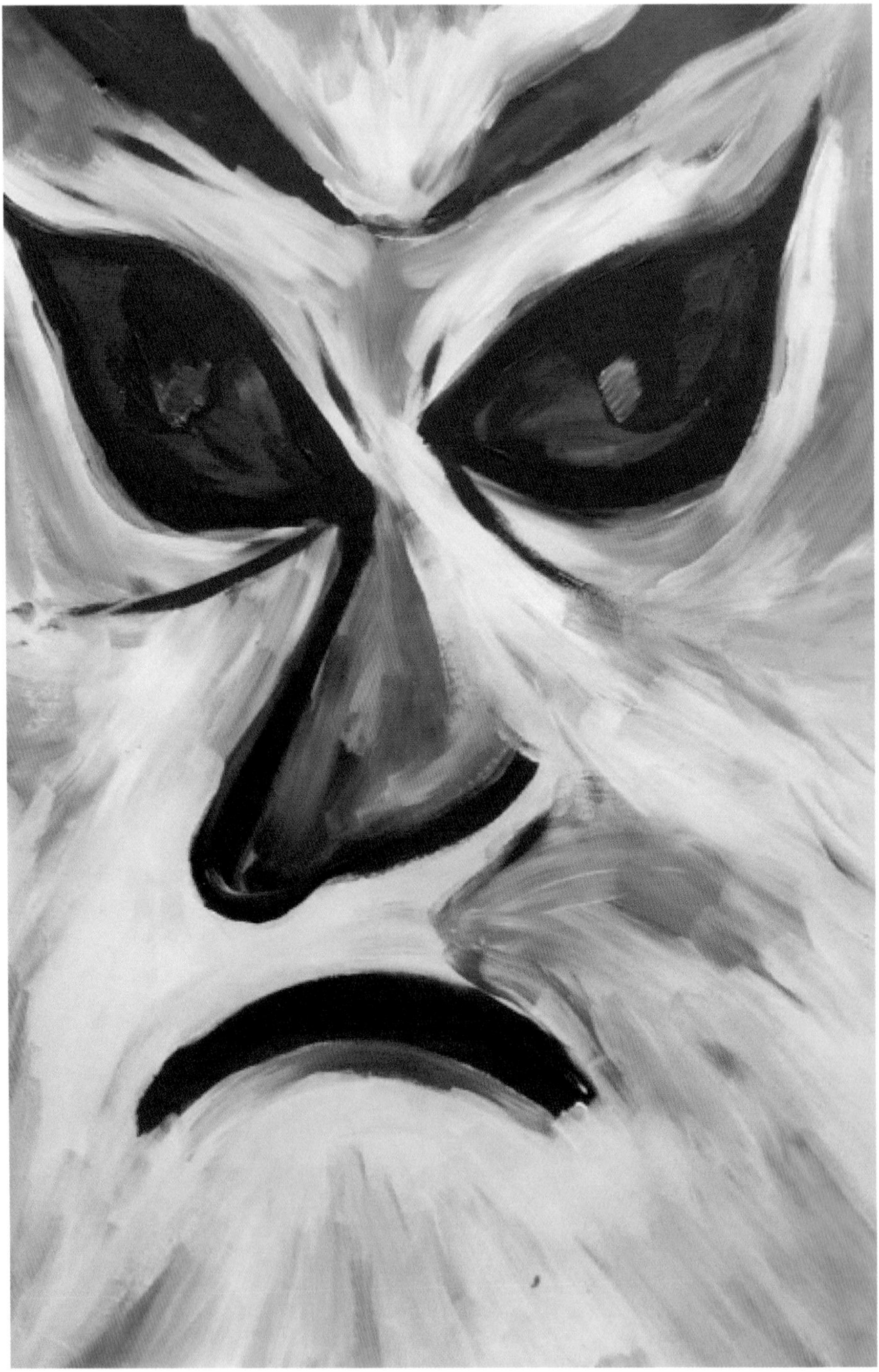

Dream Demon

I'm trapped inside a body
I feel is not my own
I am just a valley
In which his seeds are sown
He plans my every movement
And not through my own will
I follow where he leads me
Until the time to kill
Fires burn deep within me
I will not go to hell
The devil's got my body
He won't get my soul as well

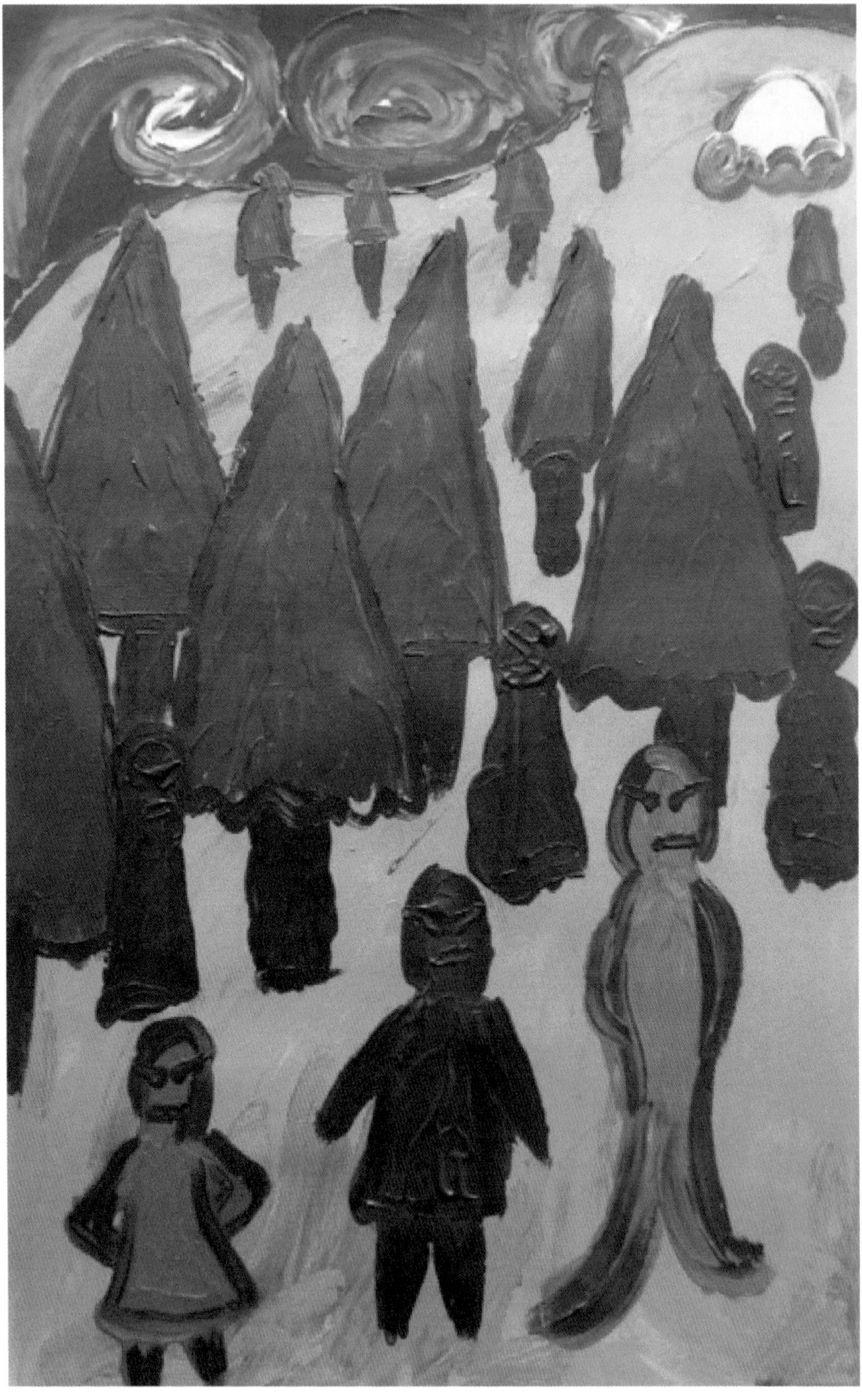

Peace

Peace, like a river
Flowing by
And where am I?
On the bank
Shaking trees
Seeking in desperation
To dislodge the truth
As it flows by
Like a river

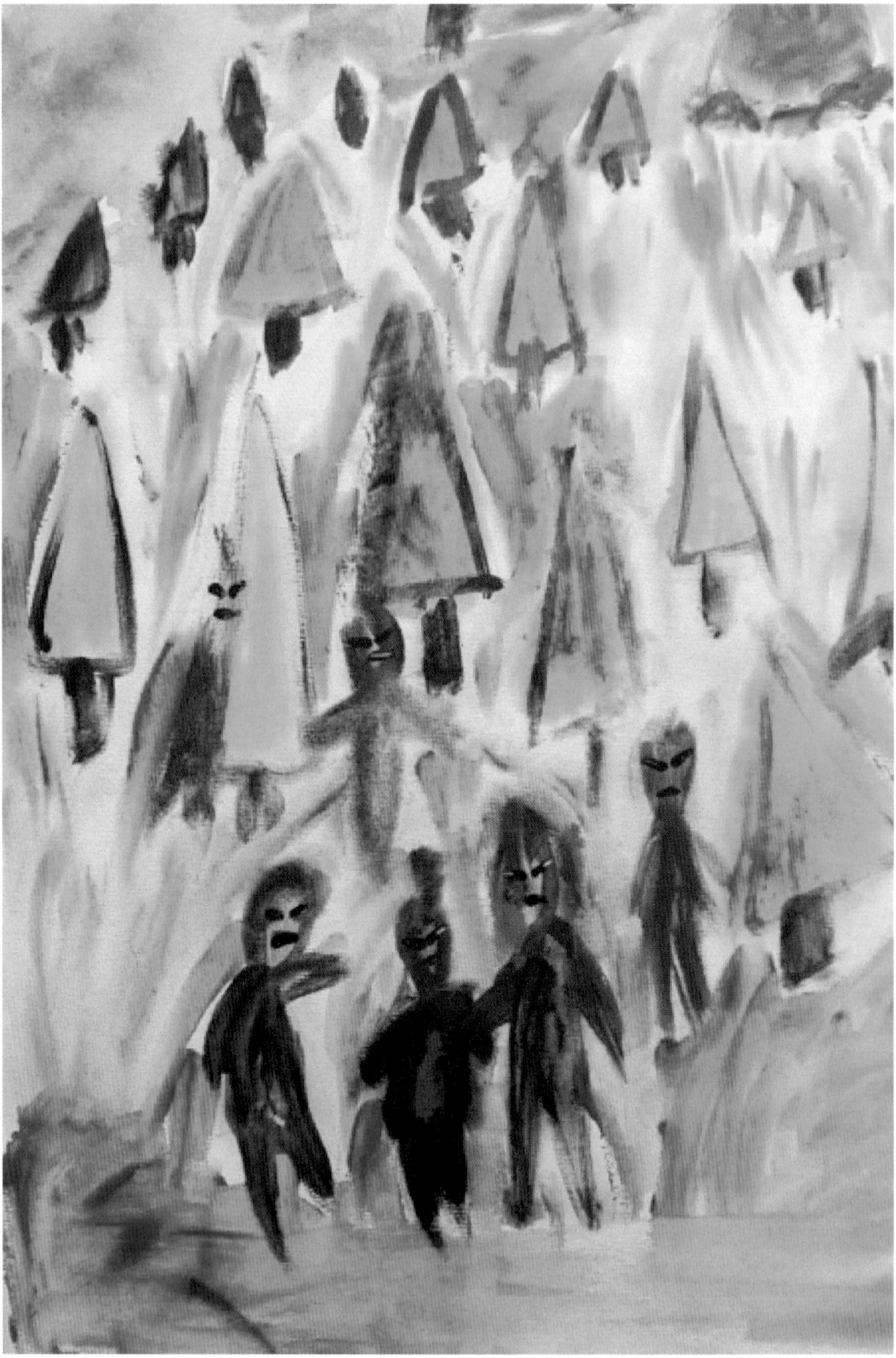

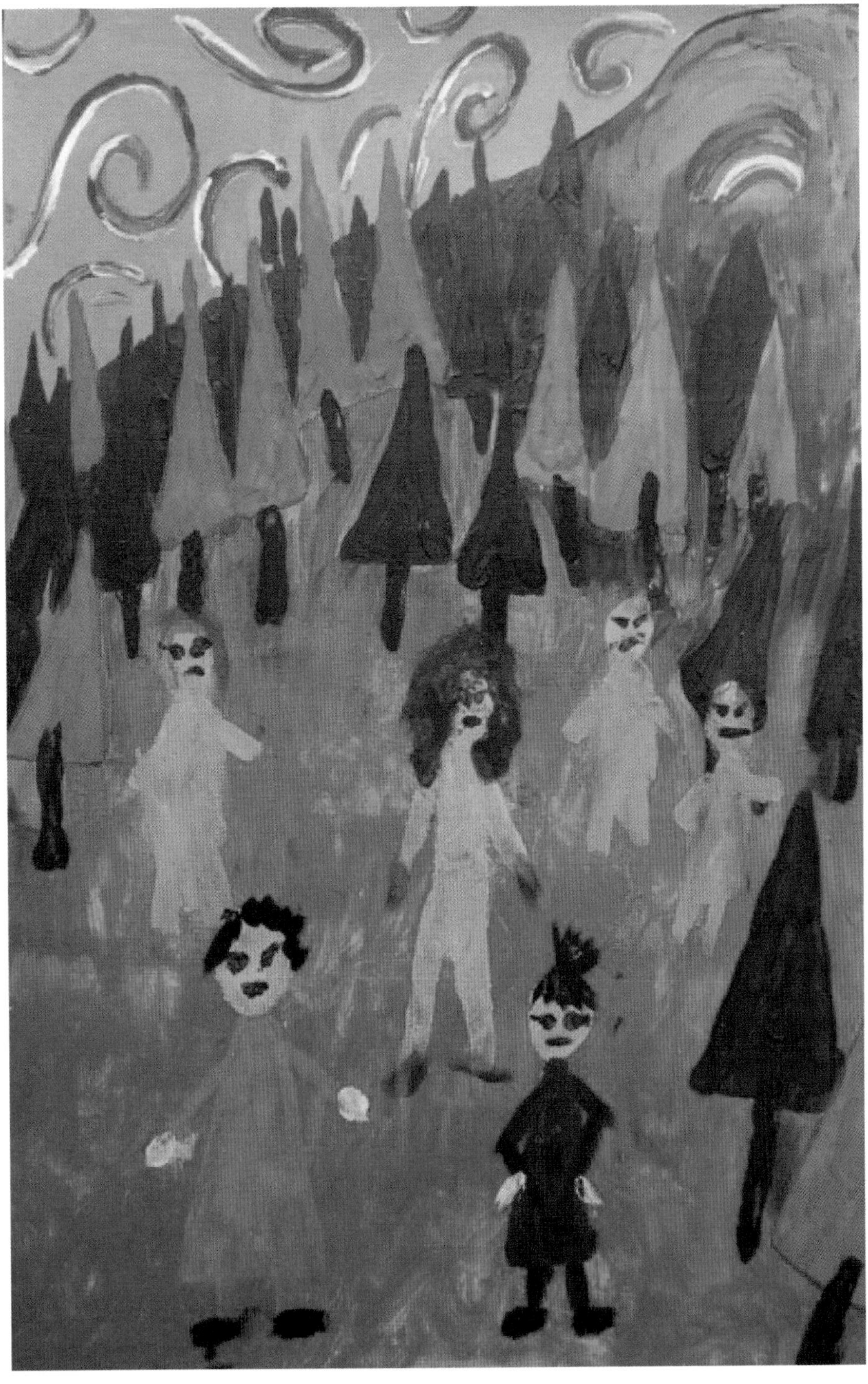

Rattle

Rattle
Snap
Turn of a key
Dying a day at a time to be free
Rattle
Drop
Pills in a pot
Amnesiac potions for time long forgot
Rattle
Shake
Pacing the floor
Desperate existence equate to no more
Rattle flail
Lost in a void
Clinging to minutes, emotion devoid
Rattle
Roll
Finding the path
Light follows dark in the aftermath

Loveless

Take me, love me, feel the burn
Second sight and deep concern
Fire forever, keep in sight
Never leaving locked in flight
Save, remember, abject fear
Bring me loveless, weeping tears
Fire in the cannon, power in kind
Never leaving, always blind

Freefall

Found myself. Only to find I was never there at all
Free fall
Colourless void. Back glance
Vibrance
Forward blur
Slur
Death of me
This setting free

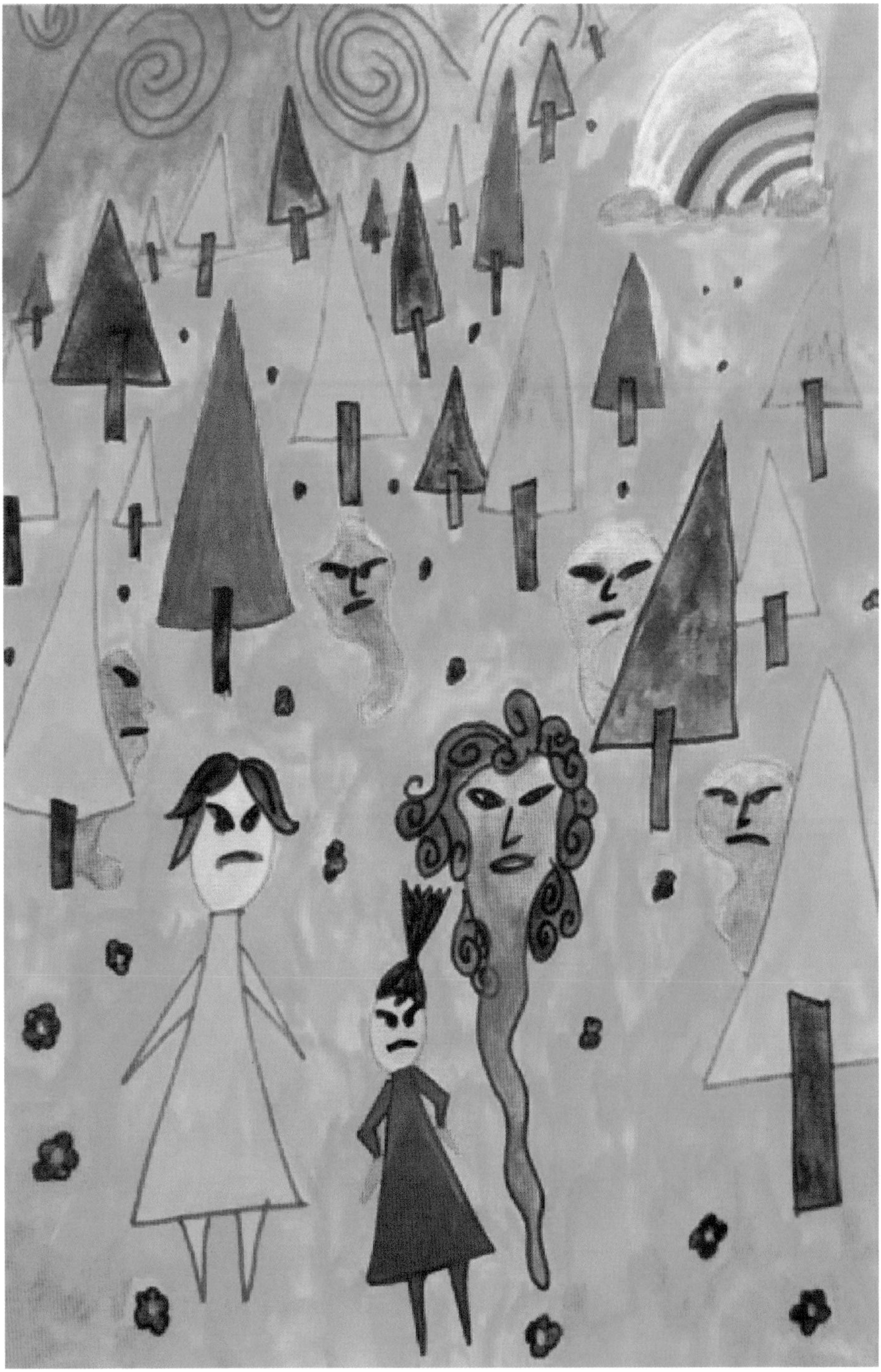

Fragments

Fragments torn
      Shards
            Broken
Liberties taken
Faking
      Healing
Feeling
Dust blowing
      Whirlpool
            Flowing
Undertow
Dragging
      Drowning
               Screaming
                 Crying
Lost, Shame, dazed

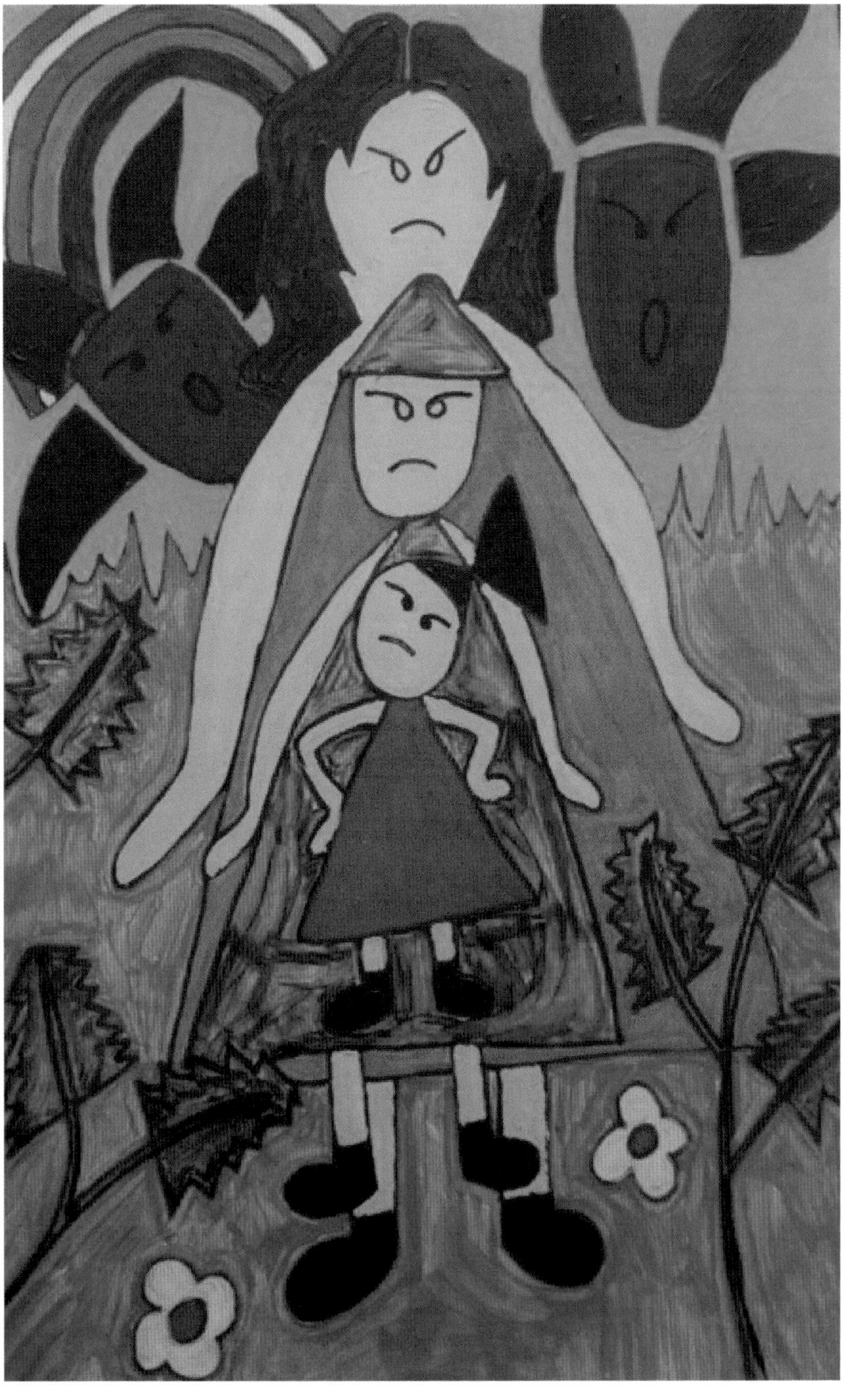

Underling

Underling. Dark thing
So big and yet so small
Eyes wide. Watching the silence
Waiting in turn. Sobering
So high and yet so low
Eyes closed. Screaming violence

Unfettered

Unfettered, I fell
Giggling. Juiced from Icarus fruits
Met a rabbit. Neon glow
Ghosts of another now then inhaled
Unchained I crawled
All fours. Fly too close to the sun
Rabbit warren. Seasonal flow
Try to contain hope sailed
Illegal, I run
Laughing, drunk on desert sands
Met a bear. Time to grow
Flight path to another now failed

Triggers came

Shook my hand
Crushed cry and stifled scream
Petrified 'til no me remained and hole's dead hands reached again
To cut the binds of tethered lies
And set the captives free

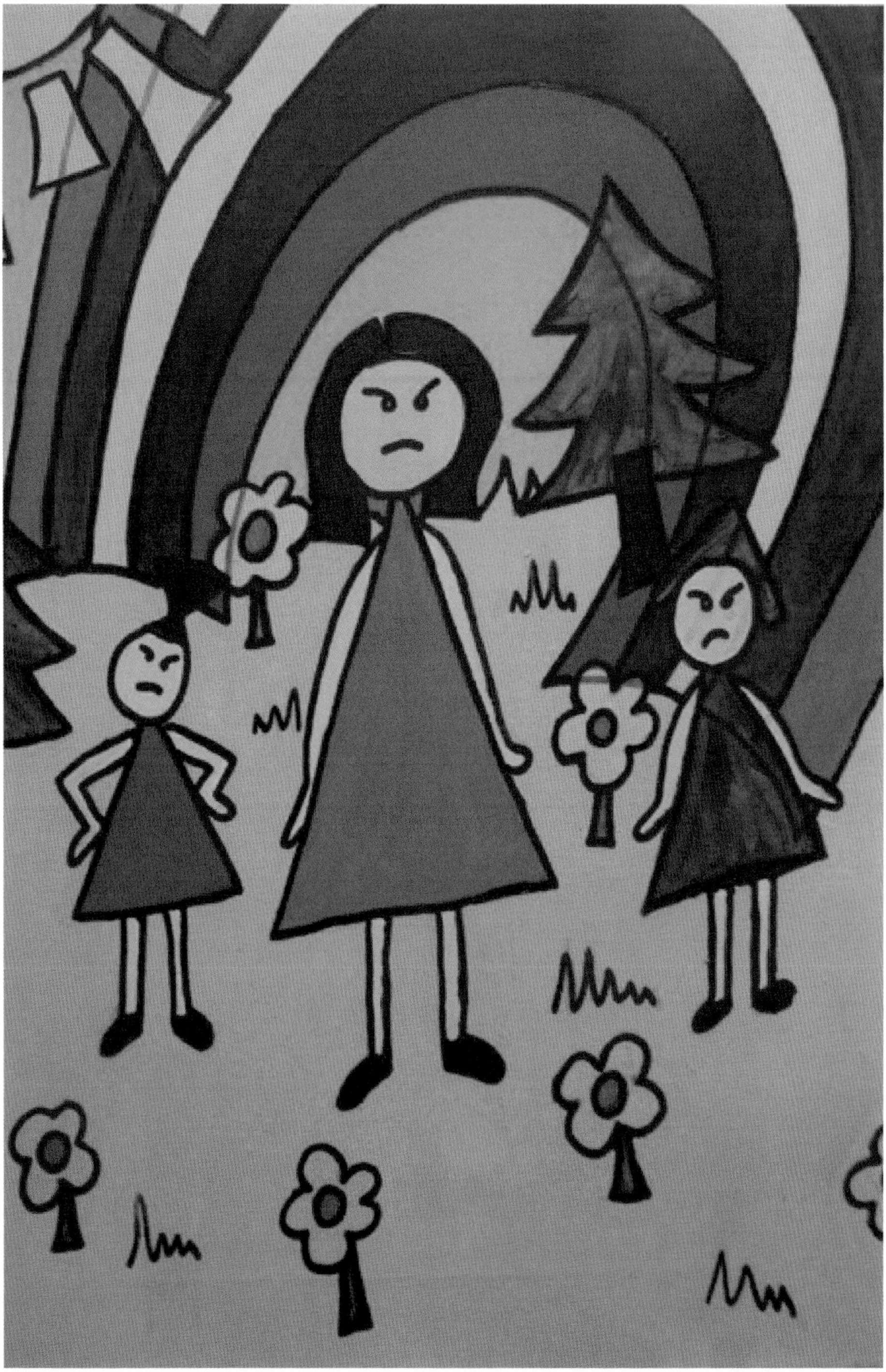

Closure

Tight, taut
'til tingling blackness
Closure
Of past and present
Of airways
Of pathways
Tight, taut

Fake

Love, hate, fear, pain
If only we weren't all insane
False scenarios, it's all lies
Everyone is so unwise

Fear, soul, fetid, blame
Cowering under septic flame
Captured memories, innocent cries
No one goes where darkness dies

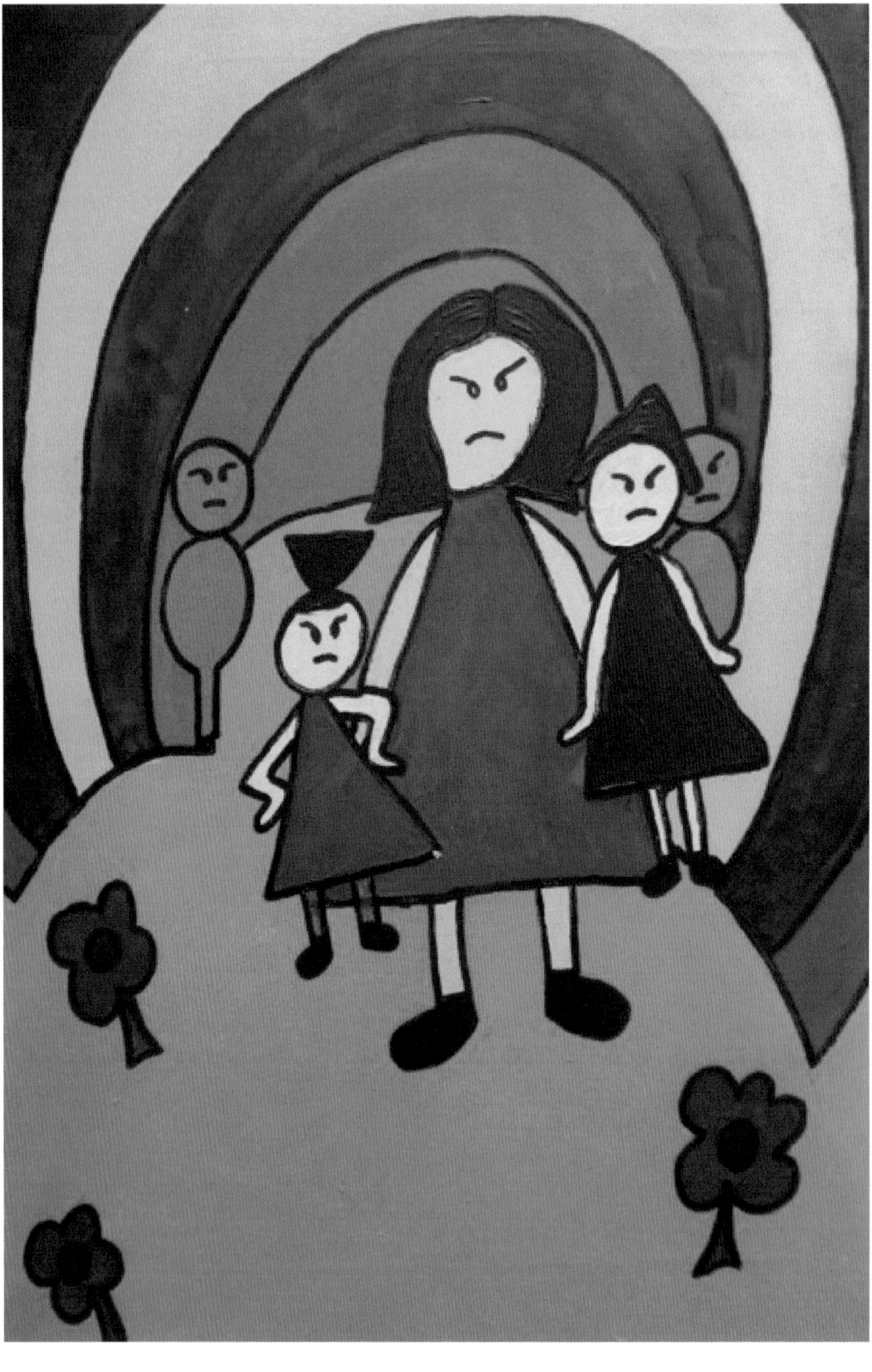

Deep

Writing
Writhing
Deep as mud
Wasting
Tasting
Stem the flood
Crushing
Crashing
Seek the good
Weeping
Seeping
Words in blood

The Family

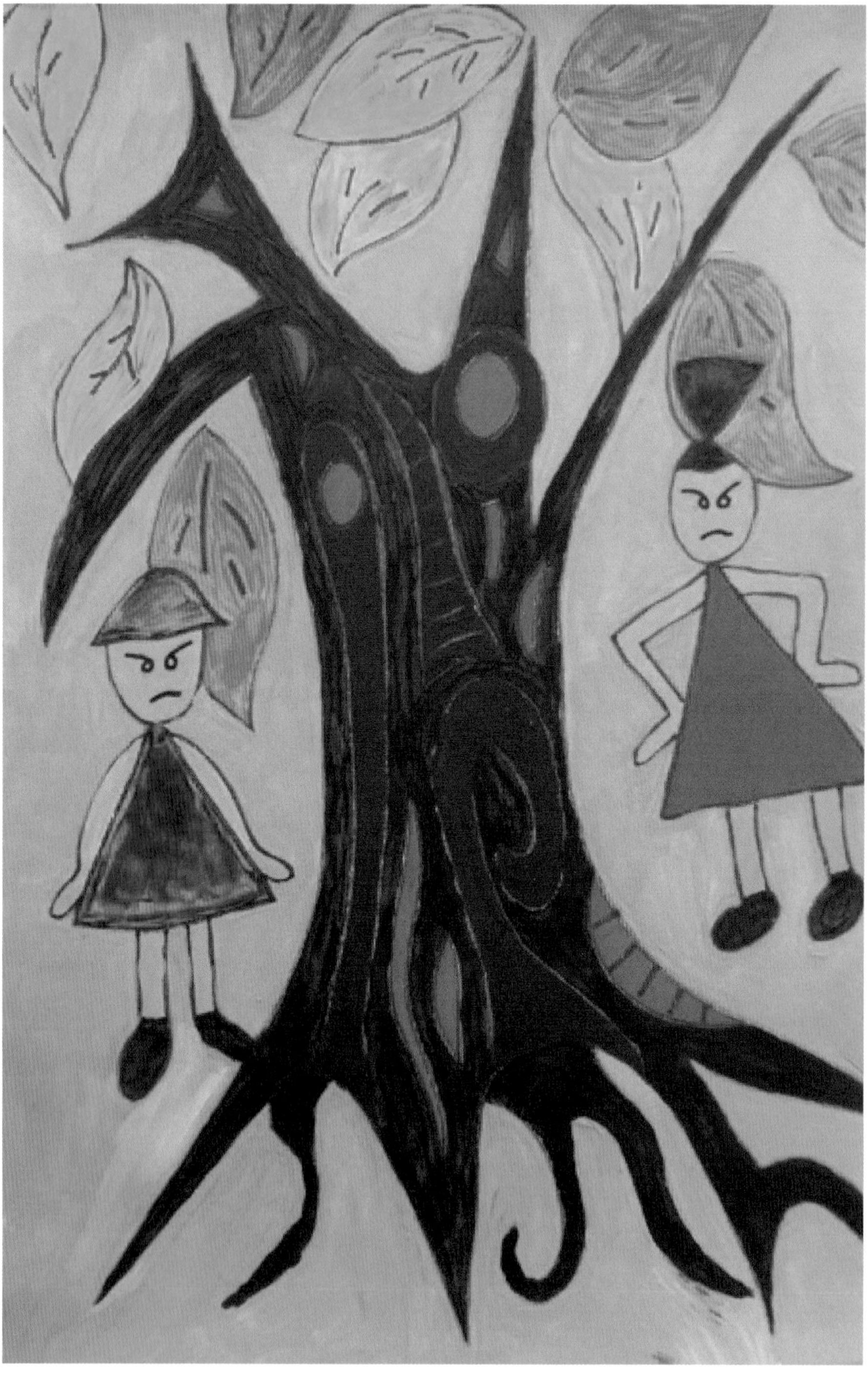

Sad

Bone tired
Achingly sad
She sits by the river
Feeling quite mad

Toes in the water
Watching the tide
Feeling like all her
Emotions have died

Grasping for feelings
Or hope which to hold
Calming her fears
And trying to be bold

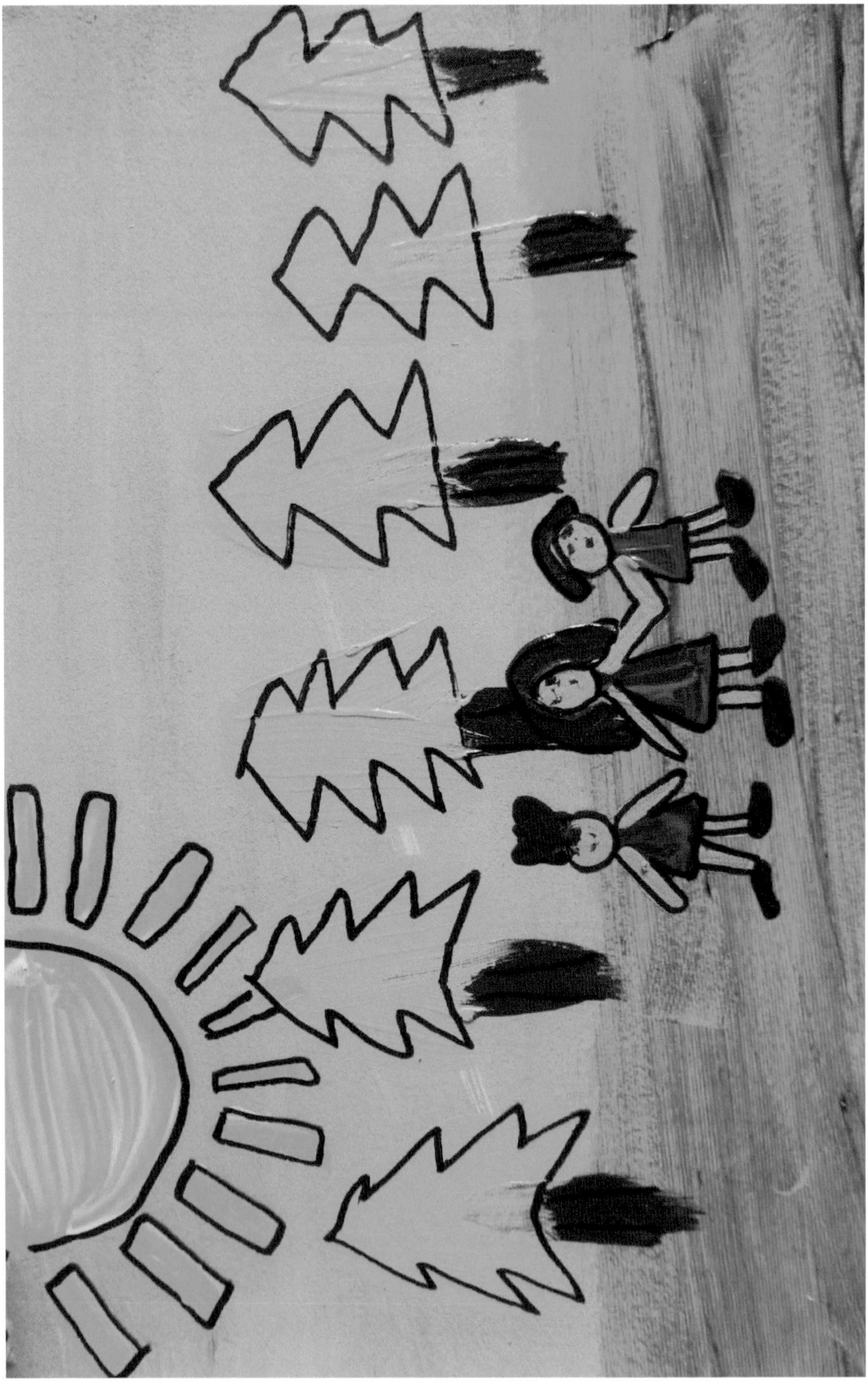

Voices

The voices call
Wanting death
Demons chatter
Thoughts a mess

The family call
And offer peace
That only comes
When you're deceased

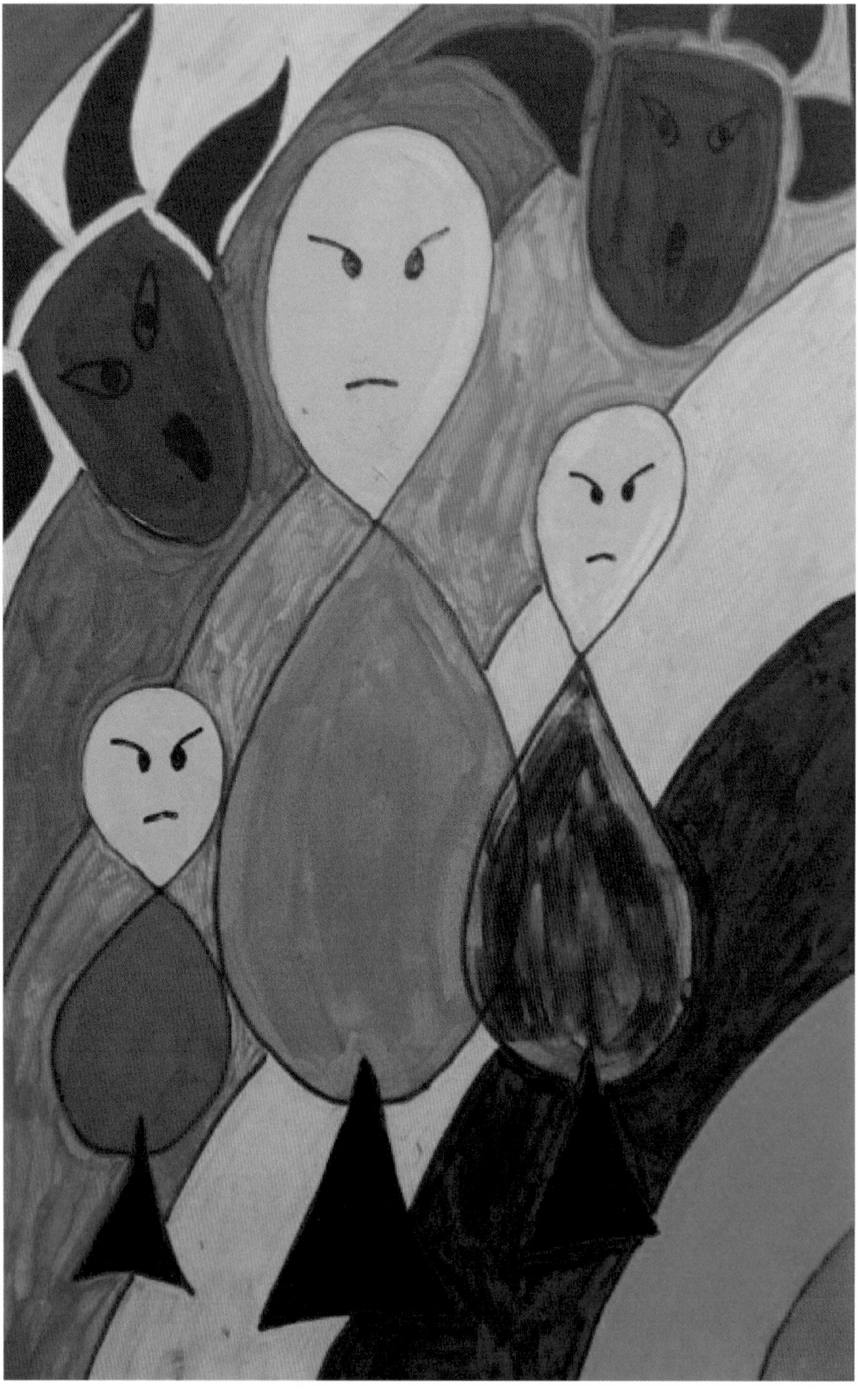

Broken

Searing
She writhes
Agony
Inside
Kill the rhyme
Just in time
Open heart
Piercing sadness
Fractured

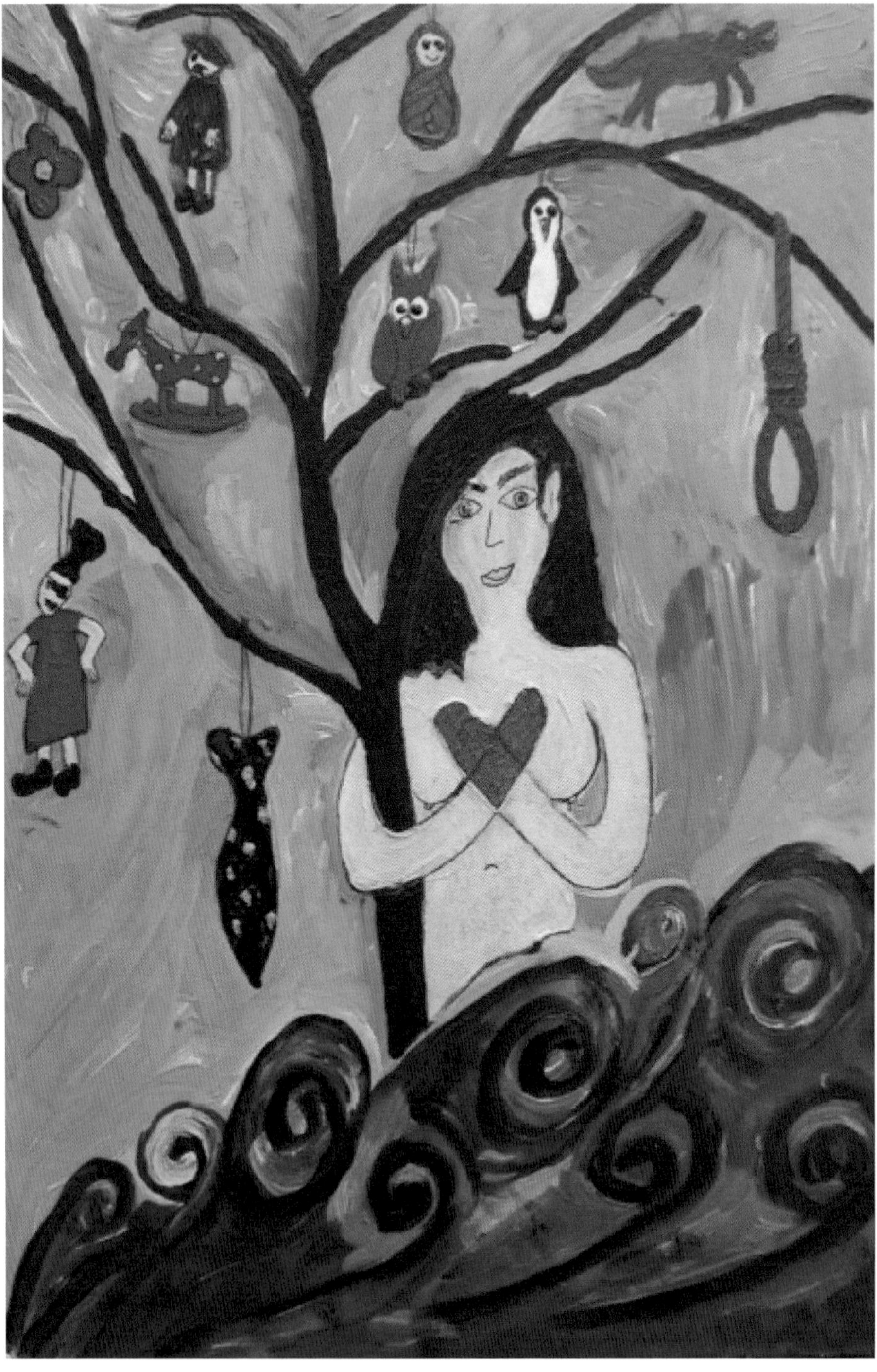

Muse

Awake again and lonely
4am and I'm starting to fall
Notepad ready and waiting
For words to come and call
Blank page, a beauty and a curse
Begging on bended knee
Slowly filling. No remorse
Muse will you marry me?
Never felt more lonely
Than at witching hour awake
With just my mind for company
What if I'm a fake
Must push on. The Family calls
I need to sit with them awhile
Page slowly filling. Rhymes all over
Fire by trial

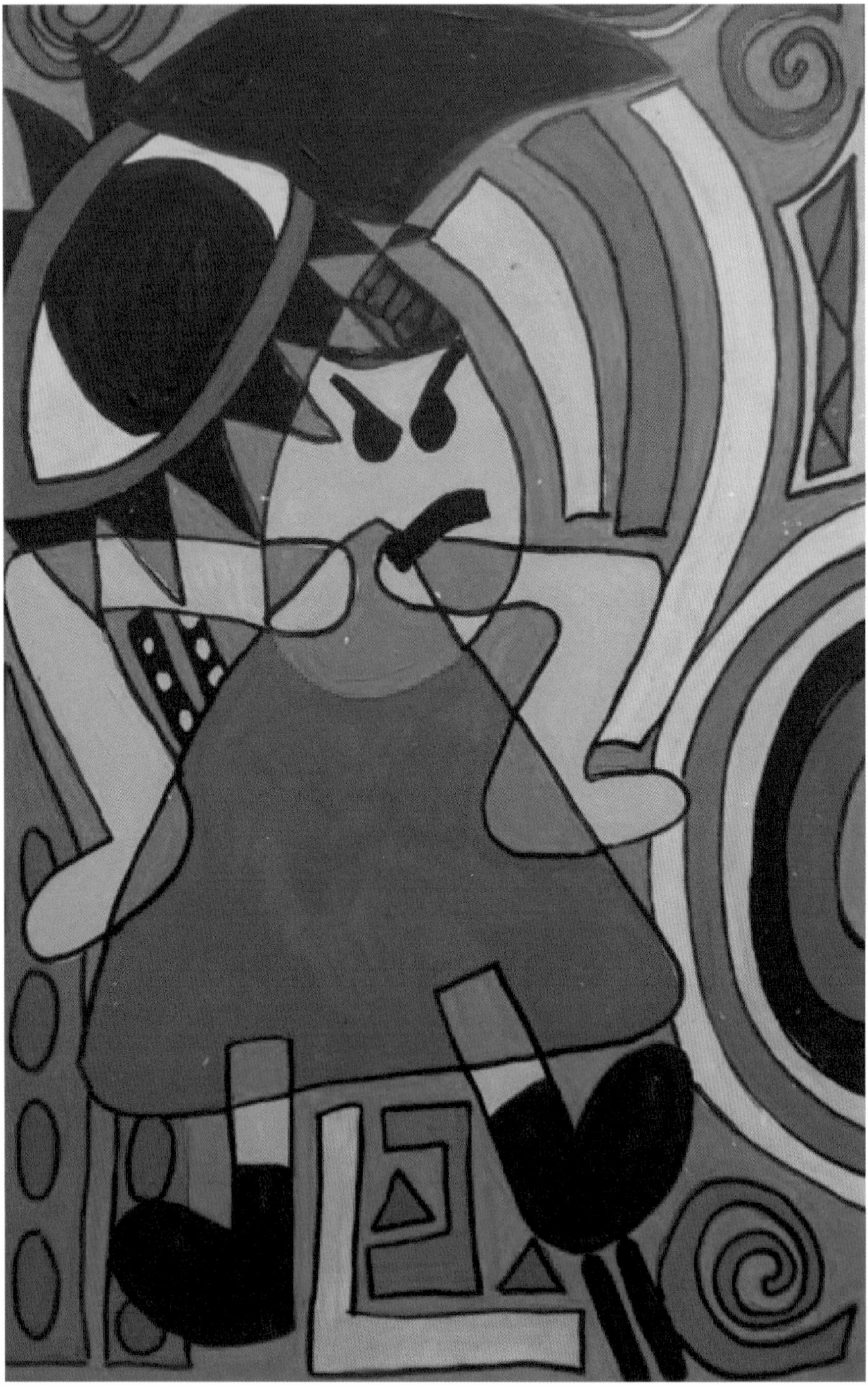

3am

3am once again, grab my paper, and my pen
The muse is strong, no sleep will come
'til all the words, on paper hum
Trucks on the highway, going nowhere
I'm safe here, without a care
The radio plays, singing to me
Hold on to life, you'll soon become free

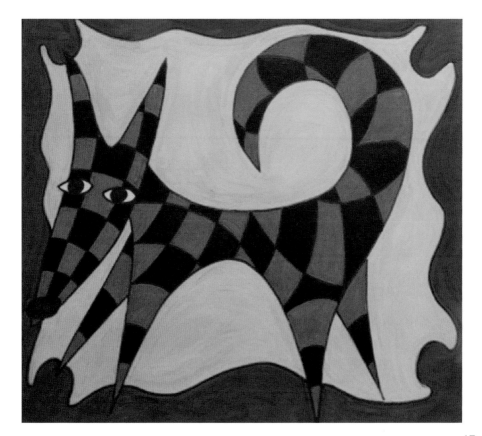

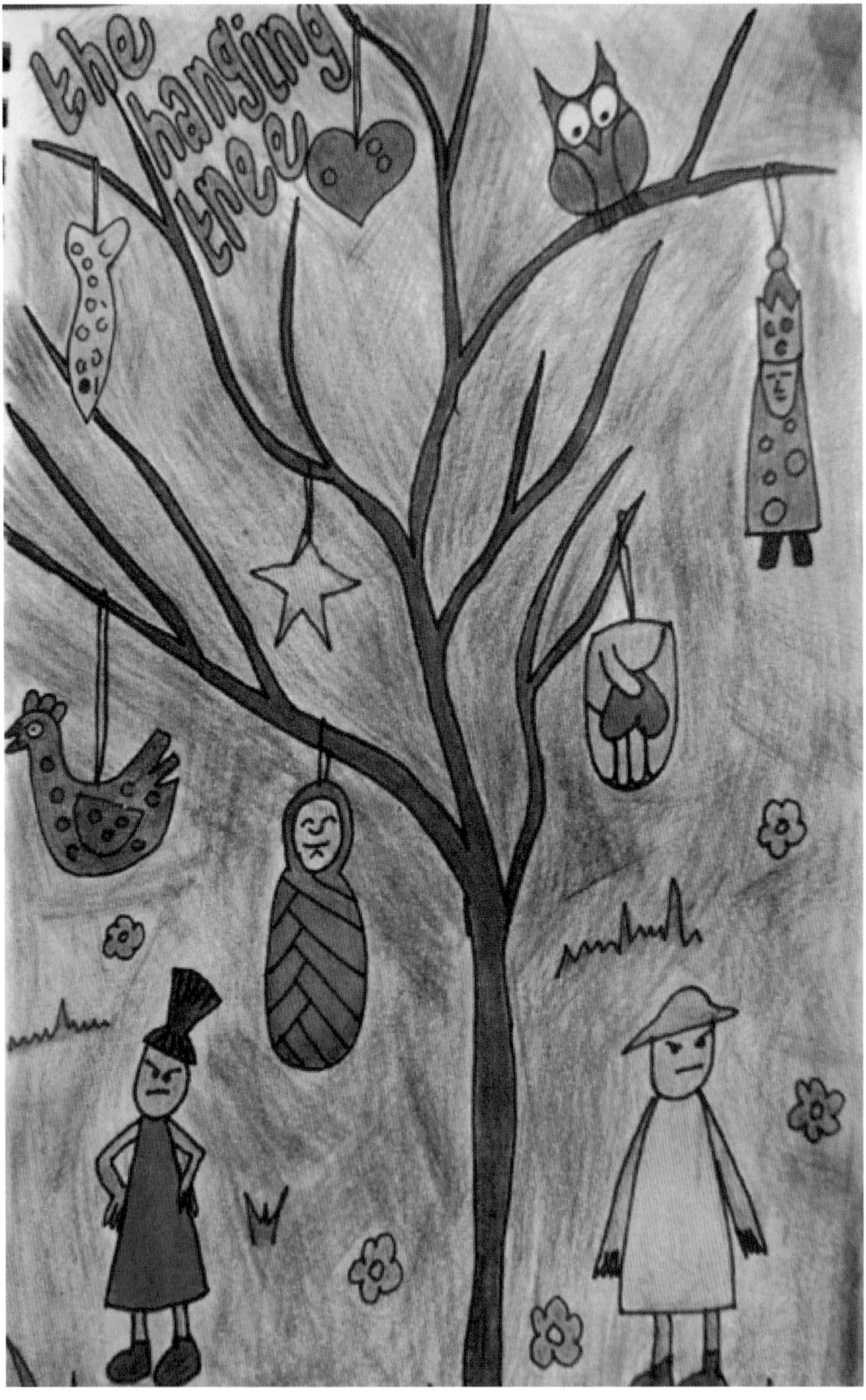
the hanging tree

Rainbow river

Beauty abounds if you know where to look
The roaring river and rippling brook
The daisy and buttercup spreads o'er the lawn
The birdsong that welcomes the rise of the dawn
Nature is great for healing the brain
Dealing with grief or easing of pain
The rainbow comes as a symbol of love
Where raindrops fall with the sun from above

The Family

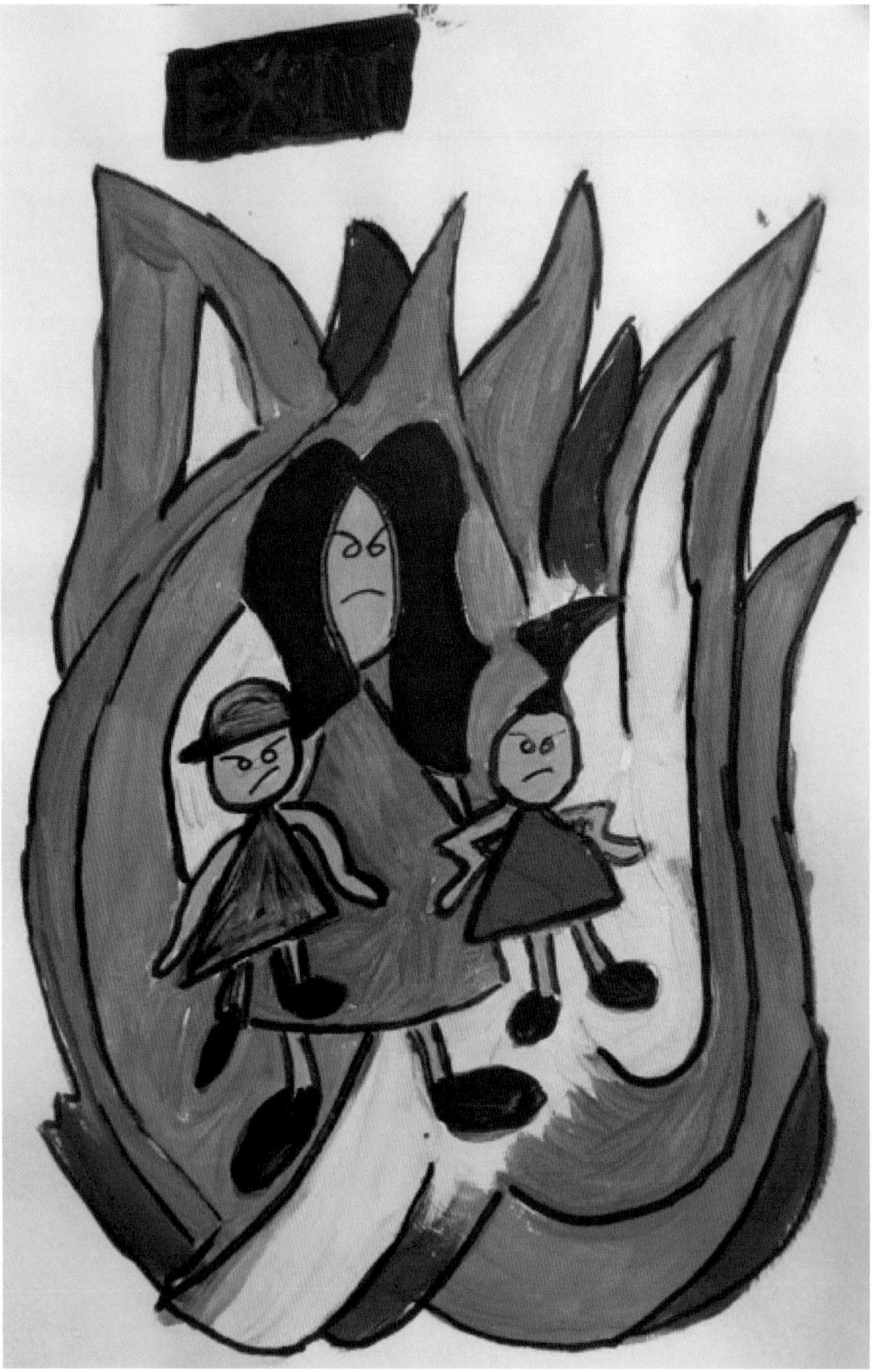
[redacted]

Between Two Worlds

Between two worlds is where we meet
Outside of my broken brain
The family group together and stand
While the demons dance in the rain

Between two worlds is a place where they live
they welcome me there too
they say I'm part of the family
and here is where I grew

Between two worlds neither here nor there
The demon creatures dwell
In the dark forests of time
Between heaven and hell

Between two worlds away from the earth
They beg of me to stay
But here and now I need to be
So they must go away

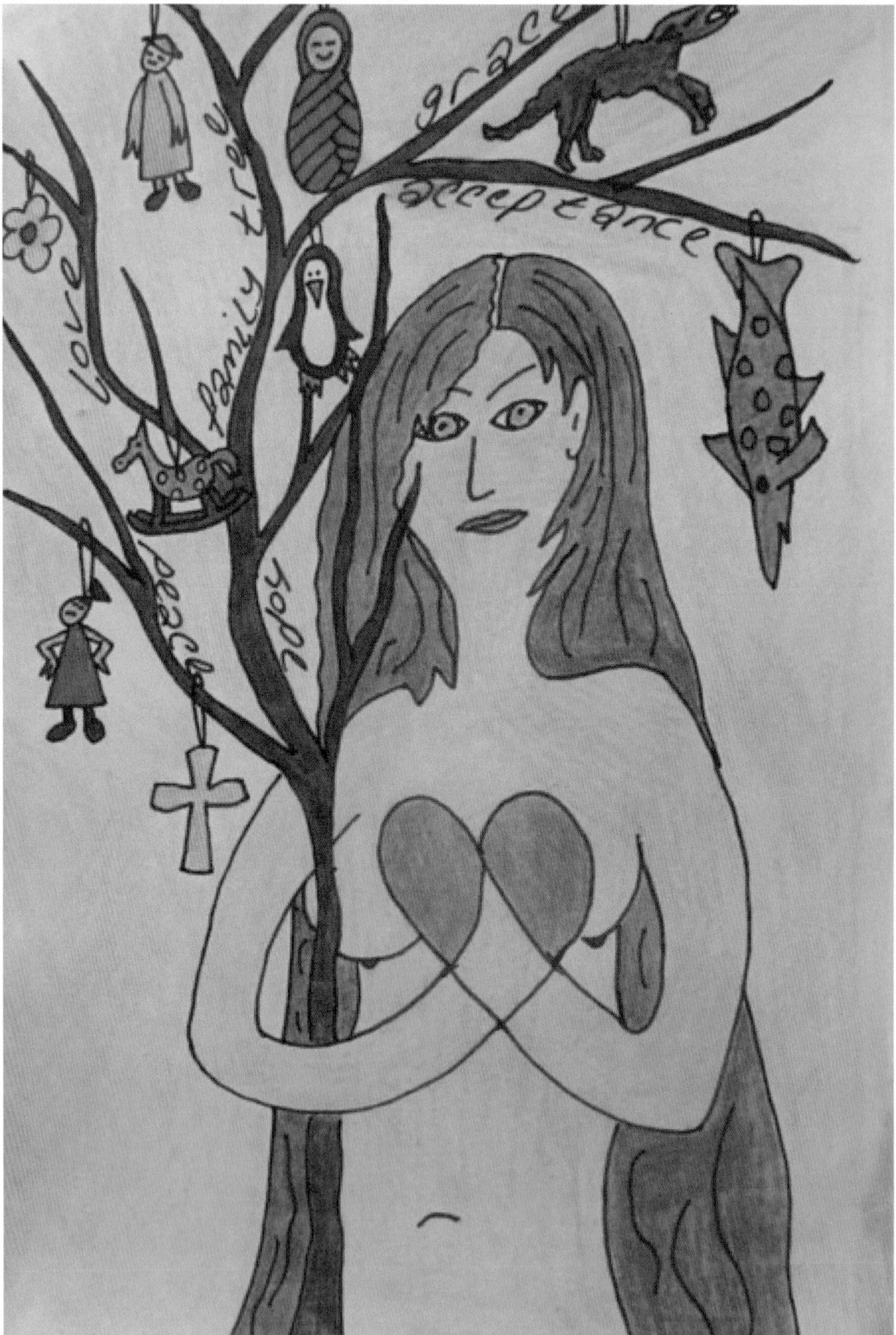
grace
family tree
acceptance
love
peace
hope

A prayer

Through a haze of drugs and discontent
You called me
From the depths of pain and persecution
You led me
Through a wave of darkness and despair
You shielded me
In a torrent of hurt and hatred
You protected me
From a life of sin and shame
You forgave me
Through a storm of tears and tantrums
You loved me
My father, I'll always be yours

The Family

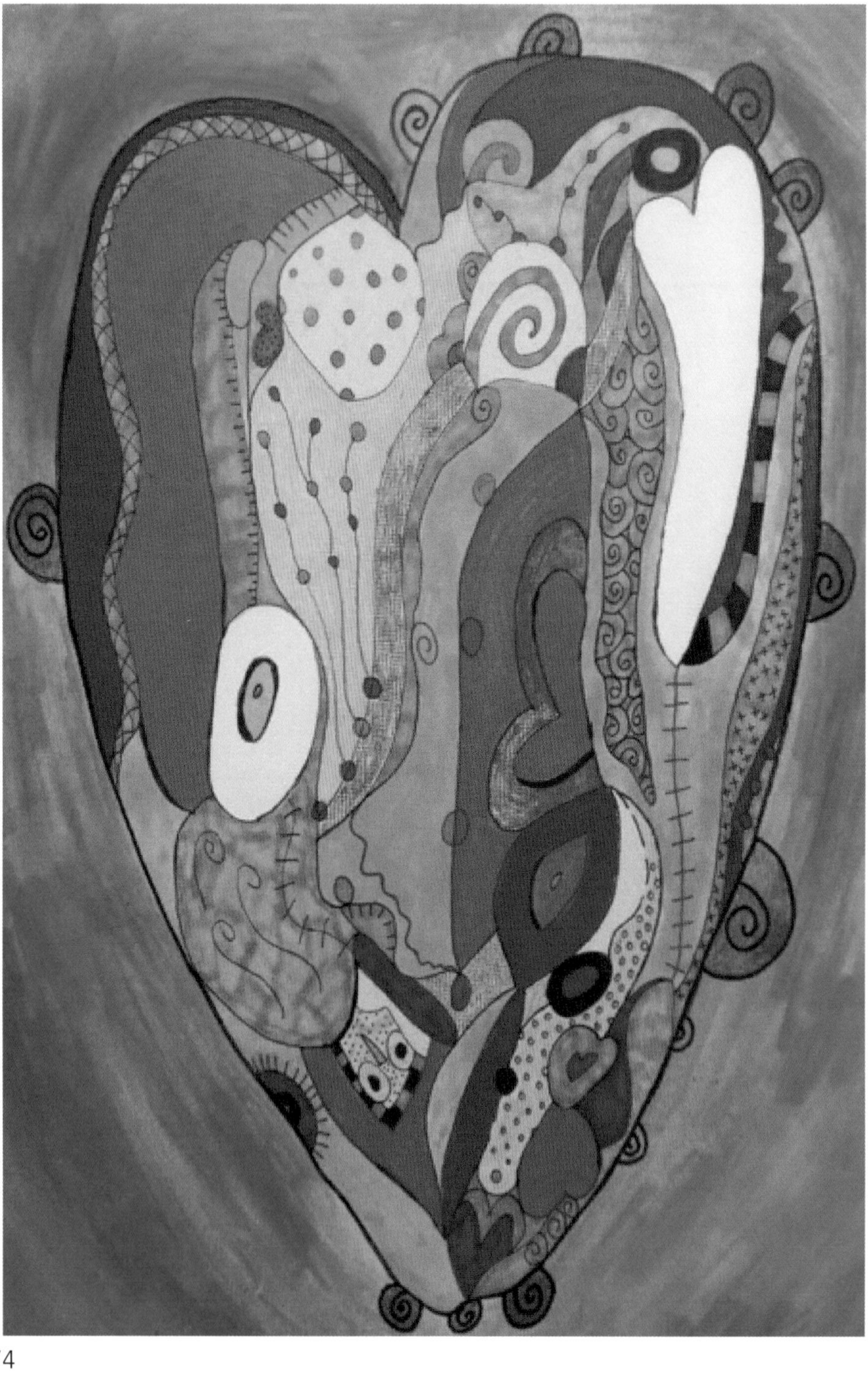

Afterword

Thank you for taking the time to experience my world. I hope it gives you a better idea of how mental illnesses can present. I still hear voices and experience losing myself to the other world that is ever present alongside ours. I've learnt to be kinder to myself and to The Family and generally they are a whole lot quieter and less of a menace. I'm now free to experiment with different types of paintings and am playing around with needle felting. I would recommend for anybody experiencing voice hearing to find some sort of art therapy as it has helped me immensely.

Other titles you may like from Motiv8.me Press

Self-care for Givers & the Helping Professions
Emma Sims, ISBN 978-1-8380546-6-3

SELF-CARE
FOR GIVERS AND THE HELPING PROFESSIONS
WHY WE DON'T AND HOW WE CAN CARE FOR OUR MIND, BODY & SPIRIT
Emma Sims

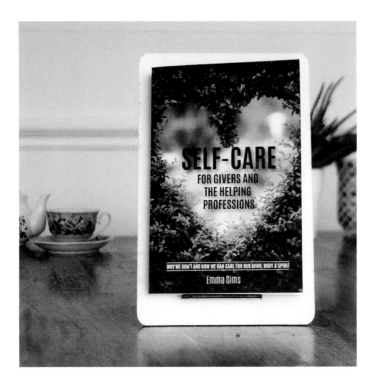

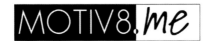

Other titles you may like from Motiv8.me Press

Reliving the Past to Release the Present
Dr. Leo Whyte, Ph.D. ISBN 978-1-8380546-0-1

RELIVING THE PAST TO RELEASE THE PRESENT
Traumatic Memories and Letters to My Younger Self
LEO WHYTE, Ph.D
"A light in the tunnel for those in darkness."

Discover more at www.motiv8.me

MOTIV8.me

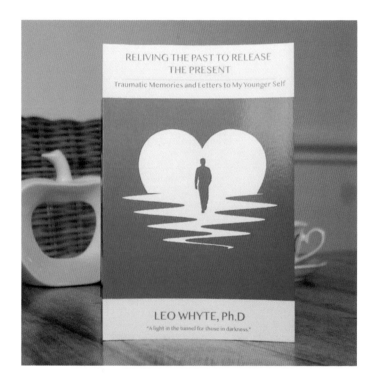

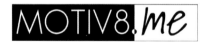

Other titles you may like from Motiv8.me Press

Life Satisfaction: A Scientist's Guide To Achieving Health, Happiness And Harmony
Dr. Leo Whyte, Ph.D. ISBN 978-1-8380546-1-8

LIFE SATISFACTION
A SCIENTIST'S GUIDE TO ACHIEVING HEALTH, HAPPINESS AND HARMONY
LEO WHYTE, Ph.D

Discover more at www.motiv8.me

MOTIV8.me

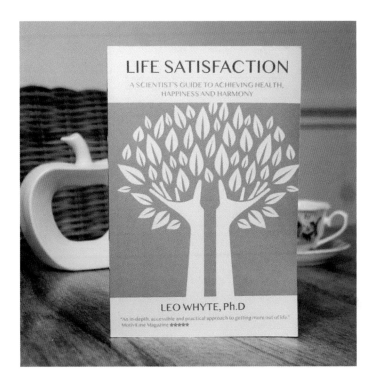

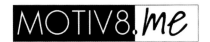

Printed in Great Britain
by Amazon

63769884R00043